ZONDERkidz **I Can Read!**™ READING WITH HELP 2

··· **MADE·BY·GOD** ···

Curious Creatures Down Under

CONTENTS

Dear Parent:
Your child's love of reading starts here!

Every child learns to read in a different way and at his or her own speed. You can help your young reader improve and become more confident by encouraging his or her own interests and abilities. You can also guide your child's spiritual development by reading stories with biblical values and Bible stories, like I Can Read! books published by Zonderkidz. From books your child reads with you to the first books he or she reads alone, there are I Can Read! books for every stage of reading:

SHARED READING
Basic language, word repetition, and whimsical illustrations, ideal for sharing with your emergent reader.

BEGINNING READING
Short sentences, familiar words, and simple concepts for children eager to read on their own.

READING WITH HELP
Engaging stories, longer sentences, and language play for developing readers.

READING ALONE
Complex plots, challenging vocabulary, and high-interest topics for the independent reader.

ADVANCED READING
Short paragraphs, chapters, and exciting themes for the perfect bridge to chapter books.

I Can Read! books have introduced children to the joy of reading since 1957. Featuring award-winning authors and illustrators and a fabulous cast of beloved characters, I Can Read! books set the standard for beginning readers.

A lifetime of discovery begins with the magical words **"I Can Read!"**

Visit www.icanread.com for information on enriching your child's reading experience.
Visit www.zonderkidz.com for more Zonderkidz I Can Read! titles.

"For in him all things were created:
things in heaven and on earth ..."

—*Colossians 1:16*

ZONDERKIDZ

Curious Creatures Down Under
Copyright © 2011 by Zonderkidz

Requests for information should be addressed to:
Zonderkidz, *Grand Rapids, Michigan 49530*

Library of Congress Cataloging-in-Publication Data

Creatures down under.
    p. cm.
  ISBN 978-0-310-72187-1 (softcover)
  1. Marsupials—Religious aspects—Christianity—Juvenile literature. 2. Marsupials—Australia—
Juvenile literature. 3. Creation—Juvenile literature.
  BT746.C74 2011
  231.7–dc22   2010039915

Editor: Mary Hassinger
Art direction: Jody Langley

Printed in China
11 12 13 14 15 16 17 /SCC/ 10 9 8 7 6 5 4 3 2 1

God made everything everywhere.

He made where you are,

and he made a place called

Australia, which is sometimes

called Down Under.

God made some special animals

that live Down Under.

One of them is the …

KOALA!

The koala is sometimes called

a koala bear.

It is not a bear.

The koala is a marsupial.

That means it has a pouch

to carry its baby, called a joey.

Koalas can be two to three
feet long and weigh ten
to thirty pounds.
They have gray or light brown fur
and good paws for climbing.

Koalas are picky eaters.
They eat only eucalyptus
leaves and do not drink water!

Koalas are nocturnal.

That means they are active

at night.

Koalas love to live in groups

but they rest or sleep about

18 to 20 hours a day!

God made another Australian
animal that lives on leaves.
It does not need a lot of water.
It is the …

KANGAROO!

Kangaroos are found Down Under.
They like to live in forests
and grassy plains called
savannas.

Kangaroos wander around their home to find good food to eat.
They live in mobs.
Each mob has a male kangaroo in charge.

Kangaroos can grow to be

six feet tall and weigh 200 pounds!

They have strong tails to help

keep their balance

and muscular legs to jump and run.

Some kangaroos can run as
fast as 25 miles an hour!
Some jump ten feet into the air!

Kangaroos have one baby at a time.

Their babies are called joeys.

Joeys are born and then go into

their mother's pouch and stay for

about eight months!

A male kangaroo is called a
buck, boomer, jack, or old man.
A female kangaroo is called a
doe, flyer, or jill.

Another animal that God
made for this special place
is the …

ECHIDNA!

The echidna (e-kid´-na) is also
called a spiny anteater.

God created them to look like a
hedgehog or porcupine.

He put sharp spines on their
skin so they can protect themselves.

Echidnas are not like a hedgehog
or porcupine for a big reason.
Echidnas are mammals that lay
eggs and make milk for their babies!

Echidnas live all over Australia.

They like deserts, forests, and hills.

As long as they find their favorite foods—

ants and termites—they are happy.

Echidnas do not have teeth.

They catch their dinner with a sticky

tongue and crush the bugs before eating.

Echidnas are nocturnal

so they eat at night.

This is similar to another

animal Down Under, the …

PLATYPUS!

The platypus is another mammal
that is special because it
lays eggs to have babies
and makes milk to feed them.
Adult platypuses eat water bugs,
shrimps, and worms.

Platypuses are called

duck-billed platypus because

they have long snouts.

It looks like a duck's bill.

They use it to help find food.

Platypuses are about as big as a pet cat.

They have water-proof fur.

That is a good thing!

They live by freshwater and

love to swim and dive.

God gave the male platypus a small

spike on his back ankles.

It is poisonous and helps him

protect himself.

God makes sure his special
creatures can take care of themselves.
Let's help his creatures all over the
world stay safe!